Reggie Jackson's
SCRAPBOOK

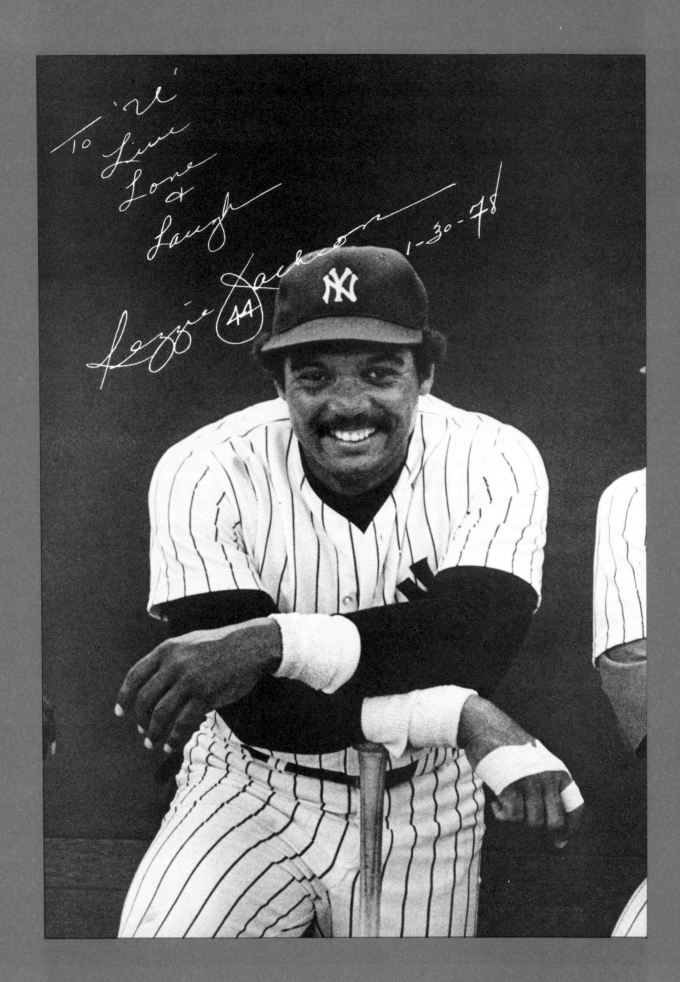

Reggie Jackson's SCRAPBOOK

BY REGGIE JACKSON

Edited by Robert Kraus

WINDMILL BOOKS
AND E. P. DUTTON
NEW YORK

Library of Congress Cata-
loging in Publication Data

Jackson, Reggie.   Reggie
Jackson's Scrapbook.
1. Jackson, Reggie—
Addresses, essays, lectures
2. Baseball players—
United States—Biography
—Addresses, essays,
lectures. I. Kraus, Robert,
II. Title III. Title: Scrapbook.
GV865.J32A56
796.357'092'4
[B] 78-2276
ISBN 0-525-61578-4 · loth
ISBN 0-525-62344-5 paper

Published in the United
States by Windmill Books
/E.P. Dutton,
New York
Published simultaneously
in Canada by Clarke, Irwin
& Company Limited,
Toronto and Vancouver

First Edition
10 9 8 7 6 5 4 3 2 1

1-30-78

A catolog of memories that helped strengthen many characters. To be enjoyed by those who stuck by me

Thanks

Reggie Jackson
44

1977 NEW YORK YANKE

First Row Seated—Bucky Dent, Roy White, Art Fowler, Cloyd Boyer, Dick Howser, Billy Martin, Elston Howard, Bobby Cox, Yogi Berra, Fred Stanley, Thurman Munson, Fran Healy, Catfish Hunter.

Second Row—Gerry Murphy (Traveling Secretary), Gene Monahan (Trainer), Graig Nettles, Reggie Jackson, Sparky Lyle, Mickey Klutts, Mike Torrez, Ron Guidry, George Zeber, Willie Randolph, Lou Piniella, Don Gullett, Ken Clay, Gil Patterson, Ed Figueroa, Cliff Johnson, Paul Blair, Herman Schneider (Trainer).

ES WORLD CHAMPIONS

Third Row—Carlos May, Ken Holtzman, Dick Tidrow, Chris Chambliss.

Seated on Ground—(Batboys), Joe D'Ambrosia, Felix Martinez, John Caldarao.

Absent From Photo—Mickey Rivers, Pete Sheehy (Equipment Manager).

JAX: REMEMBER WHAT HAPPENED TO ME

I want to tell all my friends, all our fans, everybody out there, to remember this. Remember the wonderful things that happened to me tonight, and then remember the way it was earlier. There were times when I was so low, I thought I would go crazy.

It was then that I read the Bible, and I prayed. There's a God out there somewhere. There is help there for everybody. Don't give up. Just keep moving.

This is a great bunch of guys I play with, and don't make any mistake, we were playing a great team. I don't think we saw the Dodgers at their best. I know we didn't. Ron Cey is a better hitter than we saw. Lopes is a great base stealer, but we didn't give him a chance to show his stuff. He is the real key.

Which reminds me. Give our scouts credit. They did an outstanding job. For example, when they brought in Sosa to pitch in the fourth. I got on the phone in the dugout and called Stick upstairs. That's Gene Michael, our Think Tank.

I asked him what kind of pitcher Sosa is. He told me: fastball, slider, pretty good control. I was more or less looking for the fastball on the first pitch.

They'd been pitching me inside all Series. I took a lot of them. This time, I was ready. You can pitch me in, but don't knock on the door and announce it. Even a fool can adjust.

Maybe you saw me talking to that girl in right field. I was trying to get back one of my home run balls. I offered her another one in exchange, but she wouldn't go for it. I wanted it for my father.

If you were watching TV, I know you saw me holding up one finger, then two, then three. I was doing that for my mom. I knew the camera was on me, so I said, Hi Mom, and I held up one finger. Then I hit the next one, and said, Hi Mom, and held up two. Then, the third one, and I said. Hi Mom, and held up three.

They tell me I won the car. Reporters asked me what I need with another car. Well, I have a little sister in Baltimore who can use it. Her name is Tina. She's 29. Maybe I shouldn't say that. She'll get mad at me.

I want the fans to join in our happiness. Go out and have a few drinks. Circulate the money. I'm going to give part of my World Series money to New York City, and part to Arizona, where I live, and part to Oakland, my other home. Everybody helped me get where I am; now I want to help everybody have a tunafish sandwich on me.

Of course, I'm coming back next year. I have a five-year contract. I'm a New York Yankee. Have a good winter. God bless you all.

By permission of the Daily News

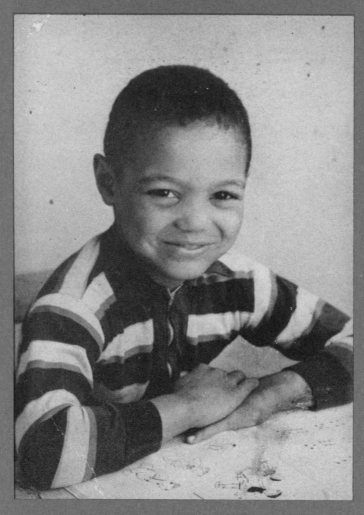

Me at 6.

I was born on May 18, 1946, in Wyncote, Pa., which is a suburb of Philadelphia. I was small as a kid—not underweight, just little. I didn't reach my full height until I was about 22.

I was a bad actor—a mischievous kid who stayed in trouble. I broke windowpanes, put mud on people's car windows—things like that. I didn't steal or rob, just a mischievous kid who liked pulling pranks.

My father played professional ball in the black league. He encouraged my interest in the game. I was 12 when I won the Most Valuable Player Award from the Little League.

This is high school baseball, sophomore year. I led the league in everything—hitting home runs, RBI's. I hit about .580 when I was a freshman and sophomore and about .550 as a junior and about .500 as a senior. I pitched too. The biggest, strongest kid in the little league junior high school always wound up being the pitcher because he was always the guy that threw the hardest and was the best coordinated. However, he didn't always have the best control.

This is me again as a sophomore at high school, a running back. I was 15 years old here.

I played freshman football at Arizona State with a guy named Curley Culp, who is now middle guard for the Houston Oilers. We had four running plays and two pass plays, but after a while it boiled down to our just getting down to the goal line, where he'd give me the ball and I'd run behind the guy named Curley Culp and we'd make our own play and that was it. I don't have any college football pictures — they were lost in a fire.

This is my junior year at Cheltenham High School. I'm 16 years old. I wouldn't have won any beauty contests that year.

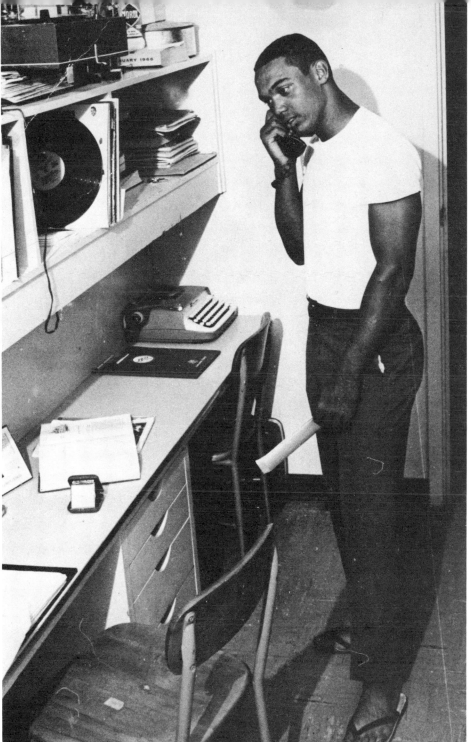

This is my room at Arizona State when I was a sophomore. Sahuaro Hall, Room 311. I'm talking to my mother on the phone. I maintained a B average. Still getting taller and just starting to get good size. This shows me in all of my glory with my five record albums and the stereo I paid $12 for and my $3 typewriter. I remember I had four pair of pants, four shirts and two pair of shoes. My older sister had bought them for me. And I was rooming with a guy named John Pitts (who played 8 years of pro football with Buffalo and Denver). Everybody used to hang around our room and watch TV. It was about a 30-inch screen—we paid $5 for it—and you had to have pliers to change the channels. It was a big deal. But fun!

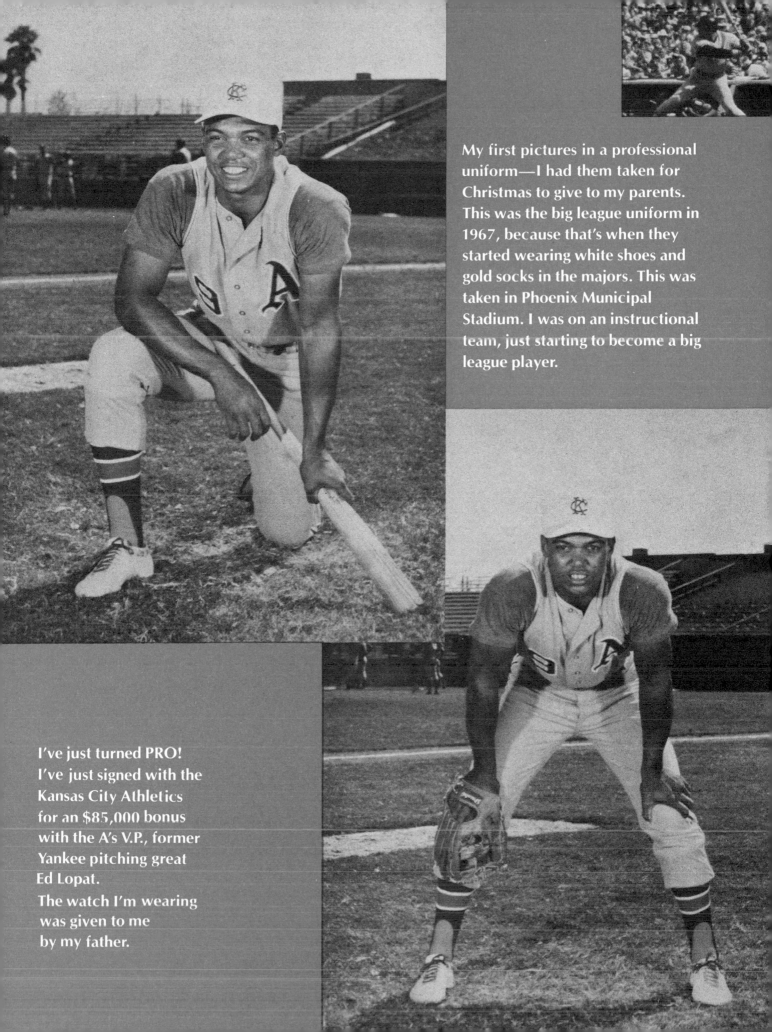

My first pictures in a professional uniform—I had them taken for Christmas to give to my parents. This was the big league uniform in 1967, because that's when they started wearing white shoes and gold socks in the majors. This was taken in Phoenix Municipal Stadium. I was on an instructional team, just starting to become a big league player.

I've just turned PRO! I've just signed with the Kansas City Athletics for an $85,000 bonus with the A's V.P., former Yankee pitching great Ed Lopat.
The watch I'm wearing was given to me by my father.

This is 1969—my second year in the big leagues, the year I was hitting all the home runs. This picture was taken in the Oakland Coliseum. I was taping my wrists because I had been hit on the hand nine times during the first half of the season. When you hit a lot of home runs, they don't like that. So they do things to try to intimidate you. When you're a young kid, they throw at you.

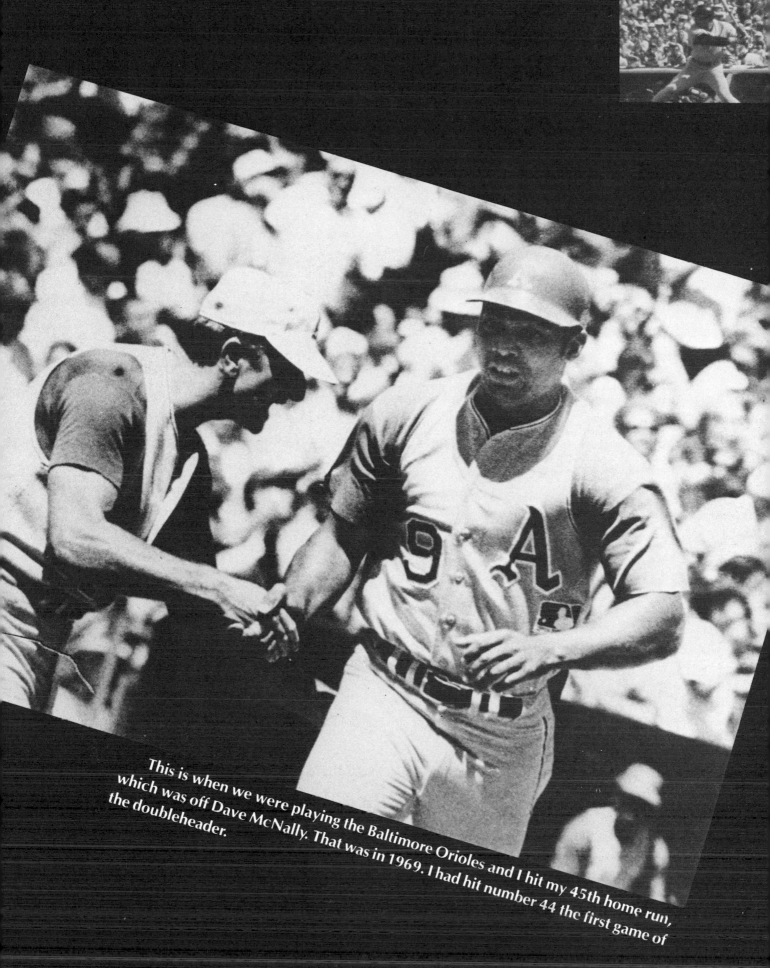

This is when we were playing the Baltimore Orioles and I hit my 45th home run, which was off Dave McNally. That was in 1969. I had hit number 44 the first game of the doubleheader.

This is in 1969 chewing bubble gum. (Kids never grow up.) I've changed to Reggie candy.

12

The All-Star game in 1971 and we are the three guys who hit home runs. Frank Robinson (left) was the Most Valuable Player. Harmon Killebrew (center) and I each hit one. This is one of my proudest pictures because it shows me with two genuine superstars. I appreciated that.

A picture taken in Yankee Stadium in 1972. Dave Duncan is on the right, I'm in the middle, and Mike Epstein is on the left. The three of us were leading the league in home runs in the first part of the season—showing the power of the A's at that time.

> **"I've had a broken neck, I've had my jaw broken in five places, been battered and bruised. In 1976 I was hit in the face."**

In 1971, '72, '73 and '74, I got hurt a lot. Because I was learning as an athlete and my body was still adjusting to my strength and style of play. I have a very physical style—I'm a laboring player, which takes a lot of physical punishment. I'm not gifted in coordination as most athletes are—I have to depend on strength. And when you do that, you tax your body. Until you learn to make adjustments by controlling how you put out muscularly, you pull muscles or have other injuries. It wasn't until 1976 and 1977 that I learned to use my strength in the right way and keep injuries to the minimum.

15

You can always tell a good swing. The hips are open and the feet are turned correctly and you have good balance, good follow-through. My head is back and my eyes are still on the ball. I'm an unusual sort of hitter. Even though I'm a lefty, I don't pull everything to right field. I have enough strength to hit a ball already past me for a home run or I can put one into the left field seats with a half-swing. The swing for a base hit is basically the same as a home run swing, but the increased power of the swing is what can take it over the fence. Most sluggers strike out a lot and I'm no exception. If you swing big, you miss big.

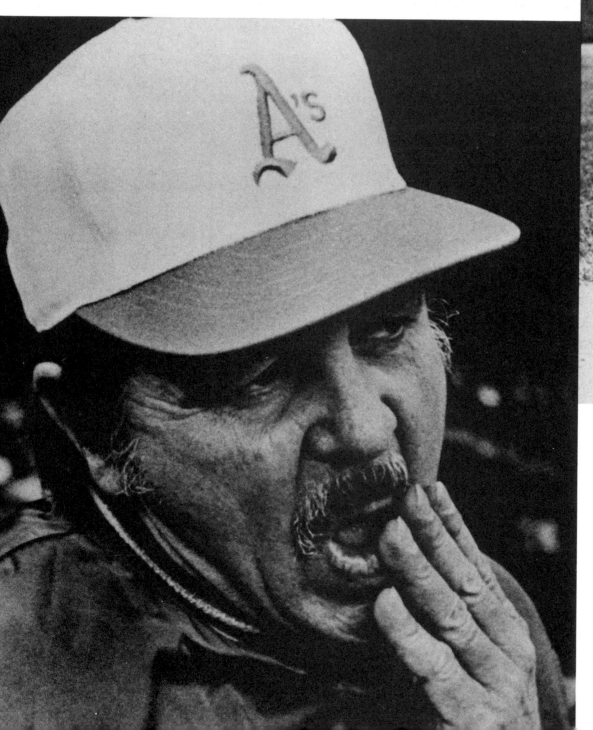

Dick Williams— the great A's manager and superb tactician. A manager and man I respect.

Here I am looking like
a twisted pretzel after
missing a pitch in the
American League play-offs
with Boston in 1975.
This looks good but no cigar.

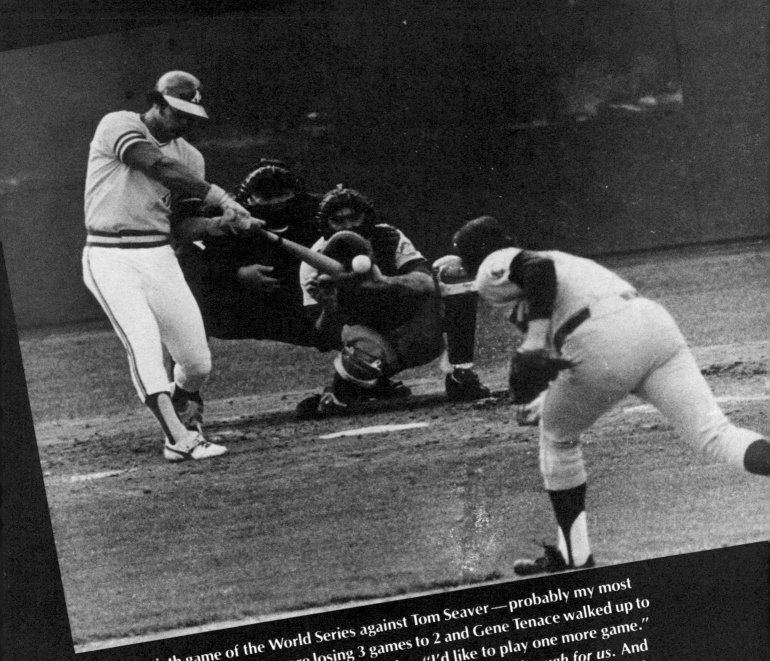

This is the sixth game of the World Series against Tom Seaver—probably my most tested moment in sports. We were losing 3 games to 2 and Gene Tenace walked up to me and said, "Buck"—my nickname was Buck—"I'd like to play one more game." Which was a nice way of saying: *Big boy, why don't you come through for us.* And Seaver was pitching. It was a tough time for us, but I had a good day. I hit two doubles and drove in two runs and scored another one, which made it 3 to 1, tying up the Series. We went on to win the next day and I was named the Most Valuable Player in the Series. In this game, I was up against the best—Tom Seaver—and I turned in the best performance I ever had up to that time.

A shoestring catch!

Commissioner Kuhn overruled Finley's attempt to release Mike Andrews from playing in the World Series. Andrews was given a standing ovation at Shea Stadium. Here you see the players giving Mike their support. This incident brought the team together.

This was a happy moment for me. I was unanimously named the Most Valuable Player of the American League of the 1973 season.

This is a 1927 Ford — it's classified as a Street Roadster and is a classic. We held the World Record in '71 and '72, and in '71 it was voted the most beautiful competition car in the world.

There is a 502-inch blown Chevy in it. It runs a B & M hydro. The motor was put together by Ed Pink and ran 9 – 9:20 E.T./148 to 152 mph. So buckle your seat belt and forget about your gas mileage.

TUNED BY
Bill Gasher

Vic Hubbard
VH
Speed and Marine
HAYWARD

MR G ASKET CO

The most satisfying thing is producing in the clutch.
Especially for someone like me, because that's when you
come under great scrutiny: *Okay, big boy, you get paid so
much, you are supposed to do —this.*

"He helped me find inner peace."

I enjoyed playing for Alvin Dark. He was one of
the most knowledgeable guys I ever played for.
He was very easy to get along with and a very
Christian man. At this stage in my career I was
just starting to settle down. I had been a
renegade for a while, but now I was developing
a philosophy about life, and Alvin Dark helped
me to find some inner peace. I just started to
become a Christian and he encouraged me and
pushed me that way. He came along to manage
our ball club at a very important time in my life
and did more for me as a human being than as a
knowledgeable baseball guy. Although as a
manager, he was outstanding. He was perfect
with the club, which he piloted in 1974–1975,
because he had players that didn't need
discipline. The only thing I'd say Alvin Dark
didn't do is discipline people, but only because
he didn't like to. He didn't like to get on
anybody's case. He didn't like to hassle anyone.

TIME

One-Man Wild Bunch

Oakland's
Reggie
Jackson

JACKSON
9

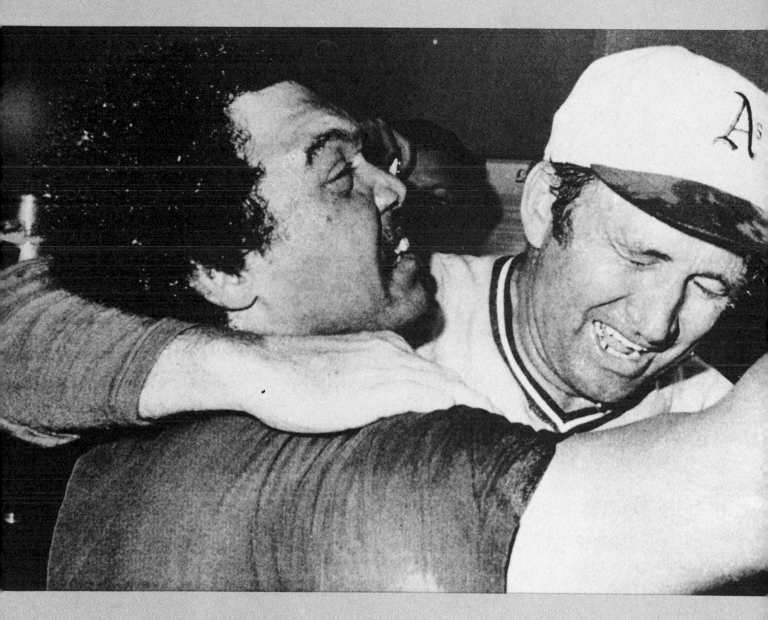

This is the cover of *Time* magazine in 1974 when I was leading the league in home runs and my batting average was like .375, .380. It was the first time an athlete made the cover since Vida Blue in 1971. This was a proud time for me.

We won our fifth straight Division Championship that year and here I am with Alvin Dark, celebrating. I've just poured champagne on him.

"I was lucky to have played for Finley."

I think Charlie Finley was a tremendous innovator and did more positive than negative things for baseball. I think he was largely involved in the free agent structure of the game. I think his failure was failure to relate to people, especially to his players—on a business level instead of as if they were his family and he was providing for them. His way was one way—and it had some merit—but in today's world it doesn't work. He had old-fashioned grit, but it backfired and he created resentments he couldn't understand. I think he is basically a good guy—the number one thing about him is that he's got a heck of a sense of humor. But he is a

"He should have hated me but played me."

businessman too, and I was lucky to learn a business philosophy from him. Finley recognized talent and put it on the field as well as anybody else I've ever played for , but here again he let personal relationships influence decisions. He traded me on a dislike, which he shouldn't have done. It would have been O.K. if he hated me but played me—he still would have won. But he shouldn't have gotten rid of me on a dislike. Which he did. But I respect him, although I'll always remember that when I played for him I had to be on guard.

"It was like breaking away from a family."

It was a very sad, lonely walk from the clubhouse to the car. The team wasn't even around. They were in Tucson and I had played so long with Oakland, from 1966 to 1976. The only thing I knew of baseball was there with the A's and I was leaving my best friends. The clubhouse people were there and tears were shed. It was very sad, very lonely and disheartening. It was like breaking away from a family. And you contemplate are you going to go, are you going to show up, do you know where you want to go. All of a sudden it is a realization and it is frightening.

That's one of my best friends, Gary Walker, waiting for me.

"I showed up a month late and nobody could deal with that."

"Being booed back then was nothing."

Here I was thrown out at second base and I was running off the field. When I got traded to Baltimore nobody could understand that at that particular time I was a free agent. I wanted to be paid a certain amount of money and I told them I wasn't going to play for anything less. And nobody believed me. They thought I was negotiating, but I don't negotiate. I say what I think is fair because I know what is fair. And if we don't agree, then we just don't agree. We don't talk. Because I know what I should command. It rubbed a lot of people the wrong way. It still does.

Hitting one for the Orioles.

I must admit Baltimore was a class organization all the way from front office to ground crew. I enjoyed the players there very much and Manager Earl Weaver is a man I'll always think highly of.

"You learn to swing at the ball when it is close with two strikes."

JAX SIGNS FOR 2.9 MILLION $

This was when we made the announcement. Here's Roy White putting a hat on me—like crowning me as a Yankee. That's Thurman Munson on my right. It's the Americana Hotel, November 29, 1976. I didn't sign the contract until January 1977—I just agreed with Steinbrenner with a handshake and never broke my word.

"Dad, you're so cute."

This is my mother and father at the announcement. They were both very proud. This was the first time I had ever had a Yankee uniform on. I wanted my family to be involved.

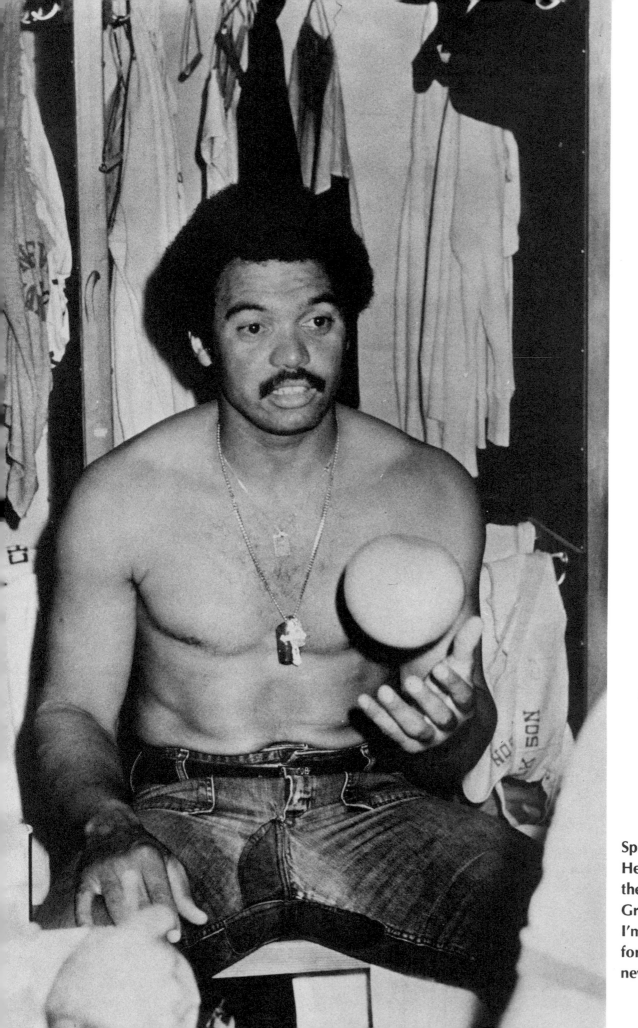

Spring training.
Here's why
they call it the
Grapefruit League.
I'm saving
for some
new pants.

This is another picture I'm very proud of. I had it framed and hung it in my house. It means a lot to me because Mickey Mantle is in it. I respected Mantle first of all. I liked him too, but I think it's more important to be respected.

Ed Figueroa

Mike Torres

Catfish Hunter

Ron Guidry

Sparky Lyle

YANKEE ACES

We couldn't have won
without Sparky. A tireless
workhorse as proven by his
Cy Young Award for 1977.
All that ability with
a Rickles-like sense of humor.

Our starting pitchers who we counted on every 4th day in 1977.

A nice man, classy guy and always a winner. Don's a friend.

Don Gullett

"They tried to pit us against each other."

Billy and I had our differences at first. It took us time to get to know each other and I think a lot of the difficulty was brought on by the press and other media. They put so much emphasis on our different personalities—they tried to pit us against each other. I think if Billy and I could have gotten to know each other without being under a spotlight or being on stage all the time we would have gotten to be friends a heck of a lot sooner. But it took us an entire season—we lived almost a lifetime in that season. And we were under such scrutiny. It is unfair to humans, but people don't understand that. I think the media took parts of his personality and parts of my personality—the grittiness, the toughness, even the loyalties—and made them into barriers between us—made both of us into brawlers, so to speak. They said we wouldn't get along. Instead of talking up our likenesses and similarities, they pitted us against each other.

The Skipper.

"His idea, his decision, his money."

George was my biggest supporter and I think he would have supported me more, but he was probably afraid of alienating more people than he already had because of me. I was his so-called bobo, I guess you could say. I was his project. It was George's decision to bring me in—his idea, his decision, his money. He pursued me. He convinced me I should come here. He signed me and he stuck with me all year. We didn't have as much contact during the season as I would have liked to have. Because of the way the papers were exaggerating how close our association was we had to stay away from each other. But we talked from time to time. I came here because of him. I thought he was a good guy. He has always been honest with me and I hold him as a man of his word, of great integrity. He has always done whatever he could for me as long as it didn't hurt the Yankees. And he is interested in helping the community and society. I know he sends a lot of kids through school. He puts seats out at the ball park to give away to the convent kids. And he has done a lot for this city just in getting this team together, in putting the Yankees back on top. I think he's treated unfairly at times—without him the Yankees would still be wallowing around. I don't think he's given the credit he should get.

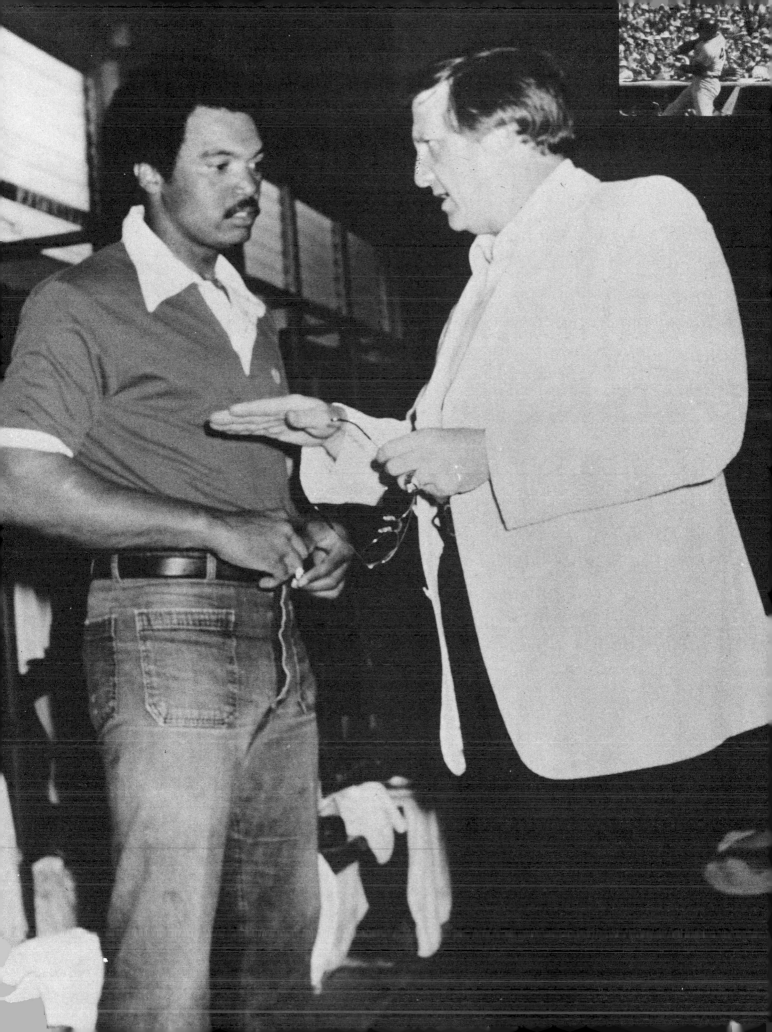

This is Thurman Munson tagging out George Brett. Thurman is the most sensitive guy I've ever played with. He's an emotional person but not in a demonstrative way. He's also the best hitter I've ever played with and I've played with Joe Rudi. Thurman is one of the quickest players around—he doesn't look it, but he has a tremendous quickness. He is a bulldog—"bulldog" is a compliment when you're talking about an athlete. He is a fearless guy and a winner. We were on our way to becoming the best of friends before some of the stories came out. He was one of my biggest supporters—my closest friend on the team.

Here Thurman Munson executes a tag-out of Frank White at home plate in the ninth inning. He was trying to score from third on a grounder to Willie Randolph.

This is Mickey Rivers, the spark plug of our offense. He makes things happen with his speed. He is an excellent pressure player and a terrific hitter. His hits and RBI's—they have meaning. They are consequential. (He's a very complex personality.)

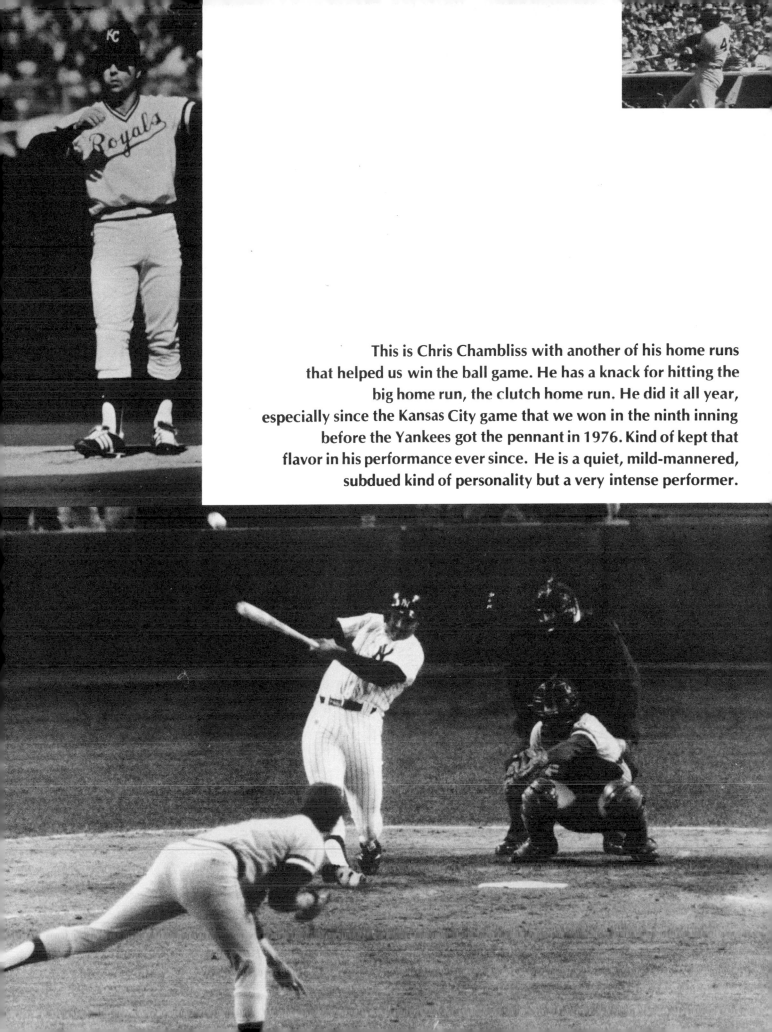

This is Chris Chambliss with another of his home runs that helped us win the ball game. He has a knack for hitting the big home run, the clutch home run. He did it all year, especially since the Kansas City game that we won in the ninth inning before the Yankees got the pennant in 1976. Kind of kept that flavor in his performance ever since. He is a quiet, mild-mannered, subdued kind of personality but a very intense performer.

Graig Nettles, to me is an underrated player. A guy who will go out and play hurt and few people will ever know it. He is a very private guy, very witty guy. He has a lot of pride in his work, and in himself. He's the best defensive third baseman I've seen outside Brooks Robinson, and the first guy I've seen that a ball park was tailored for. He is really a perfect hitter for Yankee Stadium.

Bucky Dent. He made the transition of coming here from Chicago. It was a big change for him and he did a heck of a job for us as shortstop. I think he was better in that position than people anticipated. He was an outstanding defensive player, especially towards the end when he had gotten comfortable as our shortstop. Offensively, he hit for us all year—I think he drove in around 49 runs. They were big runs and he got some big hits for us in the World Series.

Paul Blair. The ballplayer who took my place lots of times during the year defensively. He is known as the best defensive outfielder in baseball. He helped me a lot with my fielding— at a time that was difficult for me. He is a super defensive player and especially valuable to have on a team because he has played under so much pressure in the past.

This was in Baltimore. It was an exceptional warm day. I had a short-sleeve shirt on because I wasn't playing. And the people put up the $3 million hotdog sign, which was their way of showing their dislike and resentment toward what they thought were my attitudes and personality. It was all supposed to be a big put-down. But I got it all over the league wherever I went. It was a traumatic experience, a depressing, horrible thing for a man. I never want to go through it again. I wouldn't wish it on anyone. A smile covers discontent.

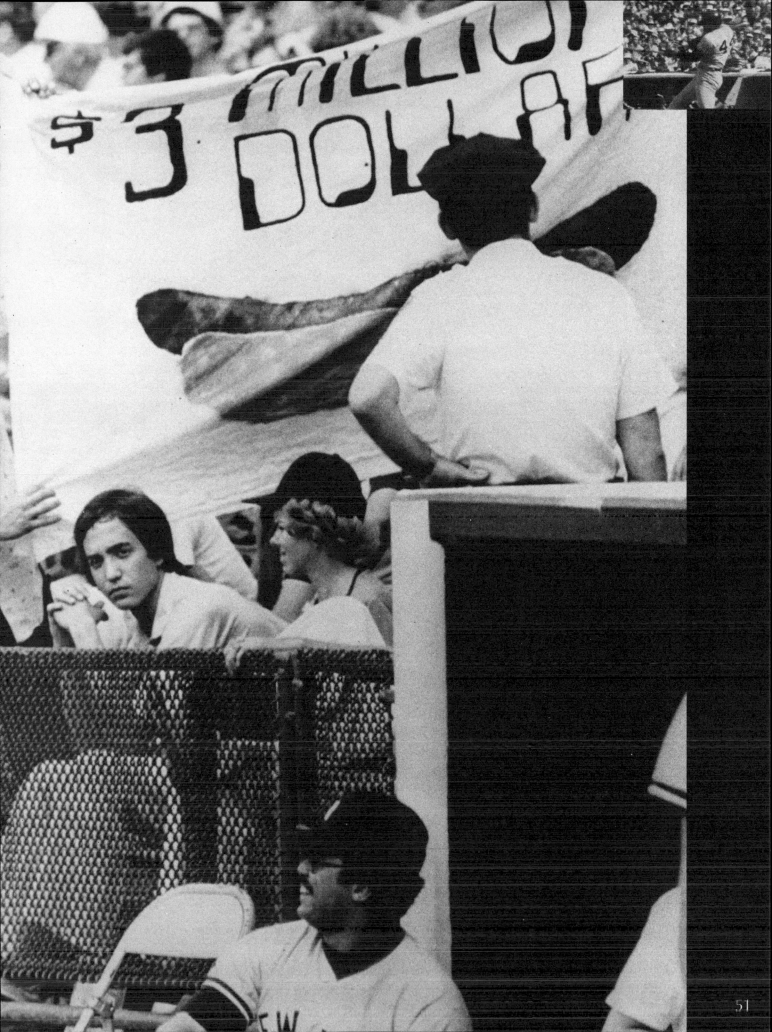

This is Doc Ellis introducing me in Baltimore. The first time we were there. I was probably treated worse here than anywhere else in my career. They threw beer at me, they hung a black Sambo, so to speak—a dummy baseball player—in right field. They threw banana skins, stones, firecrackers, eggs and apples.

"The entire team, including me, had to leave the stadium under police guard. My family could not go to the ball game because of fear."

This is a home run in Baltimore among all the boos—the worst game I ever went through. But we beat them and I got the game winning hit. Thank God.

This is Fran Healy and me. If it weren't for him, I probably would have given up fighting the whole scene, the whole soap opera, the whole baseball picture. I would have just quit. Fran gave me a different, objective picture of things that went on. He gave me a new perspective. Daily, constantly, consistently. I was lucky to have someone supporting me human to human as he did.

Willie Randolph. Willie is our second baseman. Very consistent player, very effective in the infield. He is a young man, a young player, who will clearly be the best second baseman in the league. You can probably argue whether he is the best now, but eventually he will be the best. He has fitted in well with the Yankees. A quiet, honest guy, a good Christian with a great philosophy of life. A high-quality baseball player.

I've got a
heck of an arm
most of the time.

"I was getting so much heat and hassle at the time. They had a sign about 100 yards long that said Reggie Jackson was a bad straw."

Here's Billy congratulating me after I hit my second homer of the night against the Texas Rangers on June 6.

Down but not out. This is against Baltimore in August, when I got knocked down by Jim Palmer.

"This is the way I felt almost all year
—down. But luckily finding a way
to get up and keep going."

"A home run is for a guy with a gift of strength. He uses the same swing that he would use to get a base hit but he has the strength to take that swing and hit the ball a little bit further."

61

This is me stealing a base. I had pretty good success in stealing bases. It was 17 out of 20. Being known as a slugger and a guy who doesn't run well, I made myself acquire the know-how of stealing a base. I steal with the element of surprise!

I very seldom get angry on the field, because when you get angry you lose your composure. That hurts your production—it hurts your play. It's detrimental.

You don't steal a base with speed. It is with the know-how of when to take off, who the pitcher is, who the catcher is, and the situation on the field. But I'm out here anyway.

If you let yourself flow freely you will allow your ability to create à la Dr. Julius Irving. To tell me he plans some of the artistic moves he makes is absurd. It is just that he allows his ability to create—he allows his God-given talents to do things they can do. It is just like a great writer who sits in a quiet place where he can be comfortable and then things get flowing.

"I enjoy my work!"

"A bad dream and a bad uncomfortable time."

"Some days I don't enjoy my work!"

This was probably the biggest disagreement Billy Martin and I had all year. I really came in a calm way—I wanted to know what was wrong. But Billy felt challenged, as though I had embarrassed him and the team. He wanted to show that I wasn't too big to be reprimanded or be taken out of a ball game. And when he did it, it was a show of force, of his authority. I was caught off guard. But he sights this as the turning point of the year, as the time he first stood up to me. It was part of a bad dream, a bad, uncomfortable time.

67

1977 SEASON DAY BY DAY **"THE ROAD**

Month	Date		Team	Score	Team	Score
April	7		YANKEES	3	MILWAUKEE	0
	8					
	9		MILWAUKEE	3	YANKEES	2
	10		MILWAUKEE	2	YANKEES	1
	11		AT KANSAS CITY	5	YANKEES	4(13)
	12					
	13		YANKEES	5	AT KANSAS CITY	3
	14					
	15		AT MILWAUKEE	7	YANKEES	4
	16		AT MILWAUKEE	4	YANKEES	3
	17		AT MILWAUKEE	2	YANKEES	0
	18		TORONTO	5	YANKEES	1
	19		TORONTO	8	YANKEES	3
	20		YANKEES	7	TORONTO	5
	21		YANKEES	8	TORONTO	6
	22		AT CLEVELAND	PPD.—RAIN		
	23	(1)	YANKEES	9	AT CLEVELAND	3
		(2)		PPD.—RAIN		
	24	(1)	YANKEES	10	AT CLEVELAND	1
		(2)	YANKEES	7	AT CLEVELAND	1
	25		YANKEES	9	AT BALTIMORE	6
	26		AT BALTIMORE	6	YANKEES	2
	27		YANKEES	4	AT BALTIMORE	3
	28					
	29		YANKEES	3	AT SEATTLE	0
	30		YANKEES	7	AT SEATTLE	2
MAY	1		YANKEES	7	SEATTLE	2
	2					
	3		YANKEES	8	CALIFORNIA	1
	4		CALIFORNIA	PPD.—RAIN		
	5		OAKLAND	5	YANKEES	2
	6		YANKEES	4	OAKLAND	1
	7		YANKEES	11	OAKLAND	2
	8		YANKEES	10	OAKLAND	5
	9		MAYORS TROPHY VS. METS. PPD.—RAIN			
	10					
	11		AT SEATTLE	5	YANKEES	2
	12		AT SEATTLE	8	YANKEES	6
	13		YANKEES	3	AT CALIFORNIA	0
	14		YANKEES	4	AT CALIFORNIA	1
	15		AT CALIFORNIA	8	YANKEES	2
	16		AT OAKLAND	8	YANKEES	4
	17		YANKEES	5	AT OAKLAND	2(15)

TO SUCCESS"

	18					
	19		YANKEES	9	BALTIMORE	1
	20		BALTIMORE	6	YANKEES	5
	21		BALTIMORE	4	YANKEES	3(12)
	22	(1)	BALTIMORE	5	YANKEES	1
		(2)	YANKEES	8	BALTIMORE	2
	23		BOSTON	4	YANKEES	3
	24		YANKEES	6	BOSTON	5
	25	(1)	YANKEES	3	TEXAS	2
		(2)	TEXAS	1	YANKEES	0
	26					
	27		YANKEES	8	CHICAGO	6
	28		CHICAGO	9	YANKEES	4
	29		YANKEES	5	CHICAGO	2
	30		YANKEES	5	AT BOSTON	4
	31		AT BOSTON	5	YANKEES	1
June	1		AT MINNESOTA	4	YANKEES	3
	2		YANKEES	10	AT MINNESOTA	3
	3		AT CHICAGO	9	YANKEES	5
	4		YANKEES	8	AT CHICAGO	6
	5		YANKEES	8	AT CHICAGO	6
	6		YANKEES	9	AT TEXAS	2
	7		AT TEXAS	7		3
	8		YANKEES	9	AT MILWAUKEE	2
	9		YANKEES	10	AT MILWAUKEE	1
	10		YANKEES	4	MINNESOTA	1
	11		YANKEES	6	MINNESOTA	5
	12		MINNESOTA	6	YANKEES	1
	13		KANSAS CITY	8	YANKEES	3
	14		YANKEES	4	KANSAS CITY	2
	15					
	16		YANKEES	7	KANSAS CITY	0
	17		AT BOSTON	9	YANKEES	4
	18		AT BOSTON	10	YANKEES	4
	19		AT BOSTON	11	YANKEES	1
	20		AT DETROIT	2	YANKEES	1
	21		AT DETROIT	5	YANKEES	2
	22		YANKEES	12	AT DETROIT	11
	23		MAYORS TROPHY: METS 6, YANKEES 4			
	24		YANKEES	6	BOSTON	5(11)
	25		YANKEES	5	BOSTON	1
	26		YANKEES	5	BOSTON	4
	27		AT TORONTO	7	YANKEES	6

	28	(1)	AT TORONTO	8	YANKEES	5
		(2)	YANKEES	5	AT TORONTO	1
	29					
	30		YANKEES	11	AT TORONTO	5
JULY	1		DETROIT	5	YANKEES	1
	2		YANKEES	6	DETROIT	4
	3	(1)	YANKEES	2	DETROIT	0
		(2)	DETROIT	10	YANKEES	6
	4		YANKEES	7	CLEVELAND	5
	5		YANKEES	5	CLEVELAND	4
	6		CLEVELAND	PPD.—RAIN		
	7		YANKEES	8	CLEVELAND	2
	8		YANKEES	7	AT BALTIMORE	5
	9		AT BALTIMORE	6	YANKEES	5
	10		AT BALTIMORE	5	YANKEES	0
	11		AT BALTIMORE	4	YANKEES	3
	12		YANKEES	5	AT MILWAUKEE	2
	13		AT MILWAUKEE	9	YANKEES	8
	14		YANKEES	6	AT MILWAUKEE	3
	15		AT KANSAS CITY	7	YANKEES	4
	16		AT KANSAS CITY	5	YANKEES	1
	17		AT KANSAS CITY	8	YANKEES	4
	18-20		ALL-STAR GAME: NL 7, AL 5			
	21	(1)	YANKEES	7	MILWAUKEE	0
		(2)	MILWAUKEE	5	YANKEES	4(10)
	22		MILWAUKEE	6	YANKEES	3
	23		YANKEES	3	MILWAUKEE	1
	24		YANKEES	3	KANSAS CITY	1
	25		KANSAS CITY	PPD.—RAIN		
	26		YANKEES	5	BALTIMORE	4(10)
	27		BALTIMORE	6	YANKEES	4
	28		YANKEES	14	BALTIMORE	2
	29		YANKEES	4	AT OAKLAND	0
	30		YANKEES	9	AT OAKLAND	3
	31		YANKEES	9	AT OAKLAND	2
August	1		AT CALIFORNIA	4	YANKEES	1
	2		YANKEES	9	AT CALIFRONIA	3
	3		AT CALIFORNIA	5	YANKEES	3
	4					
	5		AT SEATTLE	5	YANKEES	3
	6		AT SEATTLE	9	YANKEES	2
	7		YANKEES	7	SEATTLE	1
	8		EXHIBITION: SYRACUSE 14, YANKEES 5			
	9					
	10		YANKEES	6	OAKLAND	3
	11		YANKEES	3	OAKLAND	0
	12	(1)	YANKEES	10	CALIFORNIA	1
		(2)	YANKEES	9	CALIFORNIA	3
	13		CALIFORNIA	6	YANKEES	5
	14		YANKEES	15	CALIFORNIA	3
	15		YANKEES	6	CHICAGO	2
	16		YANKEES	11	CHICAGO	10
	17		YANKEES	7	AT DETROIT	5

18		YANKEES	5	AT DETROIT	4
19		YANKEES	8	AT TEXAS	1
20		YANKEES	6	AT TEXAS	2
21		YANKEES	2	AT TEXAS	1
22		AT CHICAGO	5	YANKEES	3
23		YANKEES	8	AT CHICAGO	3
24		YANKEES	11	MINNESOTA	1
25		YANKEES	6	MINNESOTA	4
26		YANKEES	6	TEXAS	5
27		TEXAS	8	YANKEES	2
28		YANKEES	1	TEXAS	0
29		YANKEES	5	KANSAS CITY	3
30		YANKEES	6	SEATTLE	5
31		YANKEES	5	SEATTLE	4
SEPTEMBER 1					
2		YANKEES	4	AT MINNESOTA	0
3		YANKEES	7	AT MINNESOTA	4
4		YANKEES	4	AT MINNESOTA	0
5	(1)	AT CLEVELAND	4	YANKEES	3
	(2)	AT CLEVELAND	5	YANKEES	4
6		YANKEES	8	AT CLEVELAND	3
7		YANKEES	4	AT CLEVELAND	3(10)
8		YANKEES	4	AT CLEVELAND	3
9		YANKEES	2	TORONTO	0
10		TORONTO	19	YANKEES	3
11	(1)	YANKEES	4	TORONTO	3
	(2)	TORONTO	6	YANKEES	4
12					
13		YANKEES	4	BOSTON	2
14		YANKEES	2	BOSTON	0
15		BOSTON	7	YANKEES	3
16		YANKEES	5	AT DETROIT	4
17		YANKEES	9	AT DETROIT	3
18		YANKEES	6	AT DETROIT	5
19		AT BOSTON	6	YANKEES	3
20		AT BOSTON	PPD.—RAIN		
21		AT BOSTON	3	YANKEES	2
22					
23		YANKEES	5	AT TORONTO	3
24		AT TORONTO	PPD.—RAIN		
25	(1)	YANKEES	15	AT TORONTO	0
	(2)	YANKEES	2	AT TORONTO	0
26		YANKEES	4	CLEVELAND	2
27		YANKEES	2	CLEVELAND	1
28		YANKEES	10	CLEVELAND	0
29		CLEVELAND	4	YANKEES	1
30		DETROIT	5	YANKEES	2
OCTOBER 1*		DETROIT	10	YANKEES	7
2		YANKEES	8	DETROIT	7

*   CLINCHED DIVISION TITLE

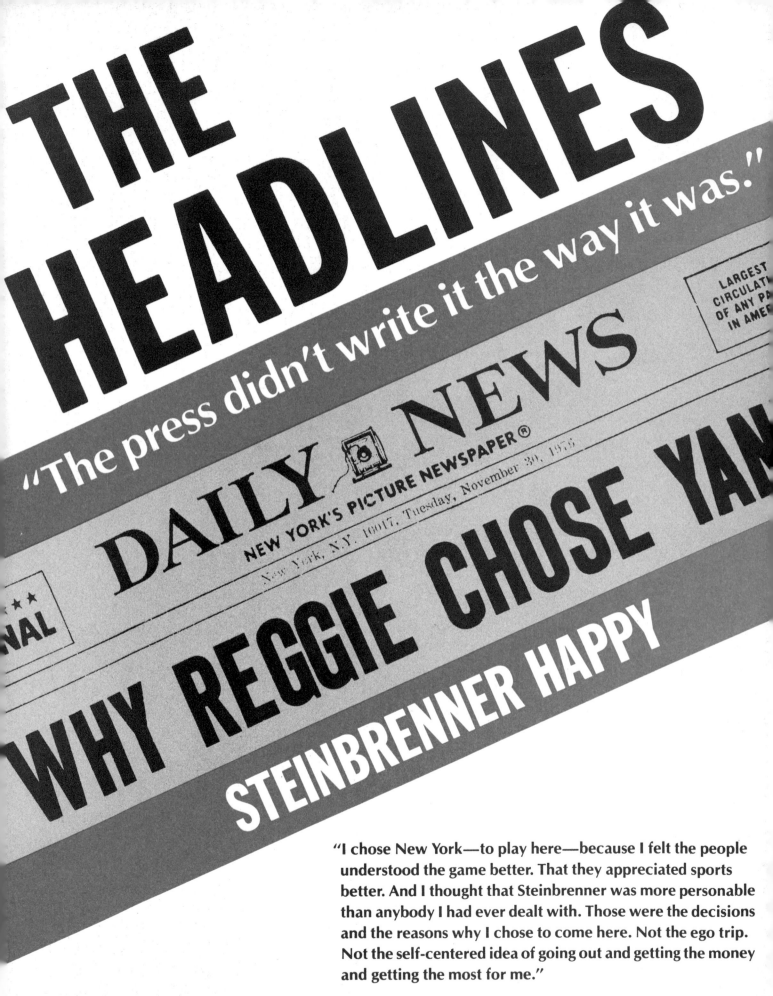

THE HEADLINES

"The press didn't write it the way it was."

DAILY ⊡ NEWS

NEW YORK'S PICTURE NEWSPAPER®

New York, N.Y. 10017, Tuesday, November 30, 1976

LARGEST CIRCULATI OF ANY PA IN AMER

WHY REGGIE CHOSE YAN

STEINBRENNER HAPPY

"I chose New York—to play here—because I felt the people understood the game better. That they appreciated sports better. And I thought that Steinbrenner was more personable than anybody I had ever dealt with. Those were the decisions and the reasons why I chose to come here. Not the ego trip. Not the self-centered idea of going out and getting the money and getting the most for me."

MARTIN FINED $2500.
MARTIN DEJECTED-SOX DOWN YAN
THE CAT'S BACK-JAX 2HRs BACK HU

YANKS SAY BILLY KE

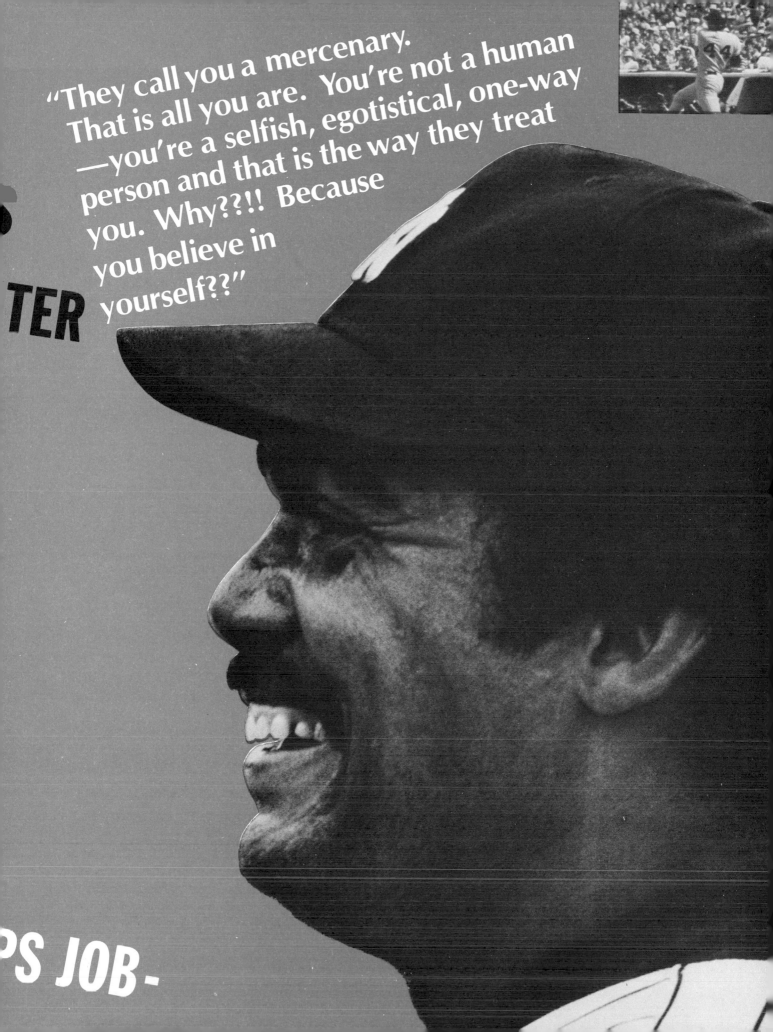

"They call you a mercenary. That is all you are. You're not a human —you're a selfish, egotistical, one-way person and that is the way they treat you. Why??!! Because you believe in yourself??"

TER

PS JOB -

BILLY & JAX

CLASH IN DUGOUT   STEINBRENNER

LECTURES CLUB;   BILLY HANGING BY

THREAD   STEINBRENNER IN CHARGE

BILLY: GEORGE SAID MY JOB IS SAFE

JAX—BILLY NOT EXACTLY BUDDIES

YANKS BOMB TRIBE   WARNS OF THE

MARTIN STANDS FIRM, SAYS HE'S

MARTIN TO YANKS: HANG DIRTY

LAUNDRY IN MY OFFICE

"People want to make
athletes different
and they are not.
They just have
certain talents."

DAILY NEWS

NEW YORK'S PICTURE NEWSPAPER®

New York, Wednesday, September 28, 1977

FINAL ★★★

YANKEES WIN IT IN 9TH, 2:

New York, Thursday, September 29, 1977

YANKEES CLINCH T E

New York, Friday, September 30, 1977

YANKS BOW, FAIL TO CLIN

New York, Saturday, October 1, 1977

YANKS STALL AGA

Kids, fans, autographs.
All connected and important to
the game and to me.

★★★★
FINAL

DAILY ⊙ NEWS

08

New York, Sunday, October 2, 1977

5 Sections

MAGAZINE COMIC

YANKS EAST CHAMPS

Champagne Bash After 10-7 Loss

Yanks: 100 Victories, 2½-Game Edge

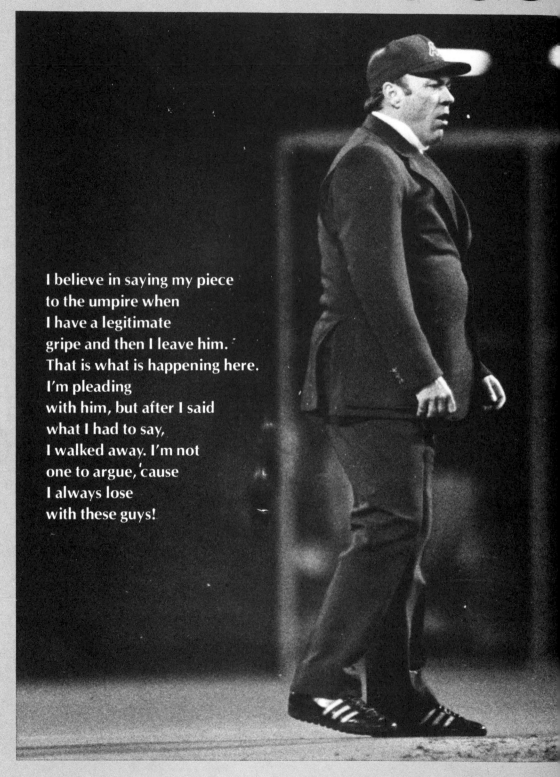

ROYALS GO

LYLE SAVES YANKEES

I believe in saying my piece
to the umpire when
I have a legitimate
gripe and then I leave him.
That is what is happening here.
I'm pleading
with him, but after I said
what I had to say,
I walked away. I'm not
one to argue, 'cause
I always lose
with these guys!

GUIDRY 3-HITT

1 UP, 7-2

KC CRUSHES YANKS; UP 2-1

-R TIES IT, 6-2

Whatta Brawl

Hal McRae's controversial hard slide on Willie Randolph. We felt that McRae deliberately did it—in order to break up a double play and let one of the runners score for Kansas. At the time this was a big, important run for the Royals and a heck of a heads-up play by McRae, but the Yankees—we disagreed with his tactic. It signaled the way the Series would be played—a very physical Series. The most physical. If one of our guys had done it—we probably would have gone along with it.

George Brett sliding into Graig Nettles at third base in Kansas City. They collided and a spat developed and then a brawl. Brett didn't like the way he was treated on the play, and Graig didn't like the way Brett slid into him. They settled it with fisticuffs.

Sitting on the bench is a pain in the butt in more ways than one. I like action and I like to play just as every athlete does. I feel I can help my team more on the field than on the bench. It took a lot of guts on Billy Martin's part to bench me. I respect him for that, even though at times I may disagree with his decisions.

This is Cliff Johnson hitting a home run with a lot of power. As much power as any guy I've ever seen. He hit 12 home runs for us during the year and Cliff didn't play a lot. The home runs he hit for us were big ones and three or four of them were in clutch situations we wouldn't have gotten out of without them. We won the division by two and a half games. That shows how important those home runs were.

Yankees 5   Kansas City 3

Winners of the American League Championship in Kansas City. That is Sparky Lyle, Fred Stanley, Willie Randolph and Thurman Munson. It was fantastic how naturally Sparky showed his jubilation.

"WE WIN!"

"THEY LOSE!"

Fred Patek, the Royals' shortstop, can't believe it is all over. People talk about the thrill of victory and the agony of defeat. In sports, people don't look at the human side of the game. They don't really know what true feelings players do have—they think we are only in it for the money—that we are only mercenaries. This is the perfect picture for showing that there is real emotion. I don't think Fred is crying—I don't think he is sad because he lost a paycheck.

YANKS ON WAY, WIN OPENER 4-3

Turmoil & Triumph: The Yanks in '77—P.82

DAILY ◉ NEWS

New York, Tuesday, October 11, 1977

72

SUTTON VS. GULLETT
Yankee Vow: No Letdown This Time

It's funny how some photos distort.
Picture reads tense. But conversation was sincere and about baseball.

91

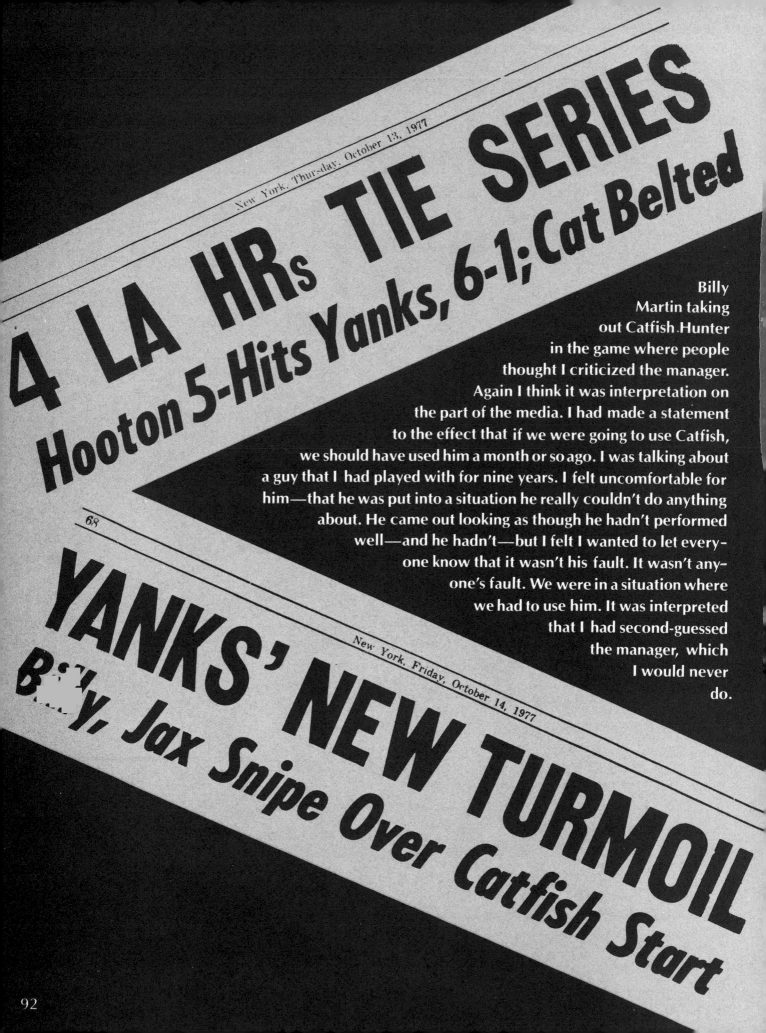

New York, Thursday, October 13, 1977

4 LA HRs TIE SERIES

Hooton 5-Hits Yanks, 6-1; Cat Belted

Billy Martin taking out Catfish Hunter in the game where people thought I criticized the manager. Again I think it was interpretation on the part of the media. I had made a statement to the effect that if we were going to use Catfish, we should have used him a month or so ago. I was talking about a guy that I had played with for nine years. I felt uncomfortable for him—that he was put into a situation he really couldn't do anything about. He came out looking as though he hadn't performed well—and he hadn't—but I felt I wanted to let everyone know that it wasn't his fault. It wasn't anyone's fault. We were in a situation where we had to use him. It was interpreted that I had second-guessed the manager, which I would never do.

68

New York, Friday, October 14, 1977

YANKS' NEW TURMOIL

B:lly, Jax Snipe Over Catfish Start

DAILY ◎ NEWS

New York, Saturday, October 15, 1977

TORREZ TERRIFIC, 5

3 Hits for Rivers; Baker 3-Run

Ron Guidry in Dodger Stadium. He really pitched a good game for us, a game we needed at the time. He was our best pitcher down the stretch and our most consistent one. The guy that we relied on. He is a small, lightweight guy—and threw about ten times harder than he weighed.

GUIDRY 4-HITS LA, 4

Yankees Soar 2 Up; Jackson: HR, D

-3

HR

Ron Cey

Steve Yeager

Reggie Smith

Steve Garvey

-2

uble

This is Ron Cey, who is a clean-up hitter who didn't have a particularly big Series against us. This was in one of their early games here in Yankee Stadium where he hit a home run. Yeager, Garvey and Cey reached the left field bleachers so easily—no one else reached them all year long against us—we were almost frightened at first. Cey was a clean-up man—110 RBI guy. Steve Yeager was an outstanding defensive catcher. Reggie Smith had a heck of a World Series. He is shown here hitting a low inside fastball for a home run. To me Steve Garvey was the most consistent player and the best all-around player. A legitimate superstar. A clutch performer, an outstanding performer, a model player, a model human being. He is great for the game.

"You get used to swinging and miss-
ing. It is all part of the job. But don't swing
and miss too much or you won't have a job."

"Home run hitters strike out a lot."

There's a lot of joking and ribbing in baseball.
Here's a little deadpan humor with
Thurman and Steve Yeager at Dodger Stadium.

I said if I ever
played in New York
they would name
a candy bar after me—
and by golly
they did!

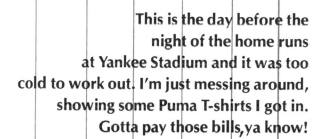

This is the day before the
night of the home runs
at Yankee Stadium and it was too
cold to work out. I'm just messing around,
showing some Puma T-shirts I got in.
Gotta pay those bills, ya know!

This is in Dodger
Stadium catching a fly
ball, on Sunday after-
noon, the day we got
the heck beat out of us.
We lost 10 to 4.
I catch most of 'em.

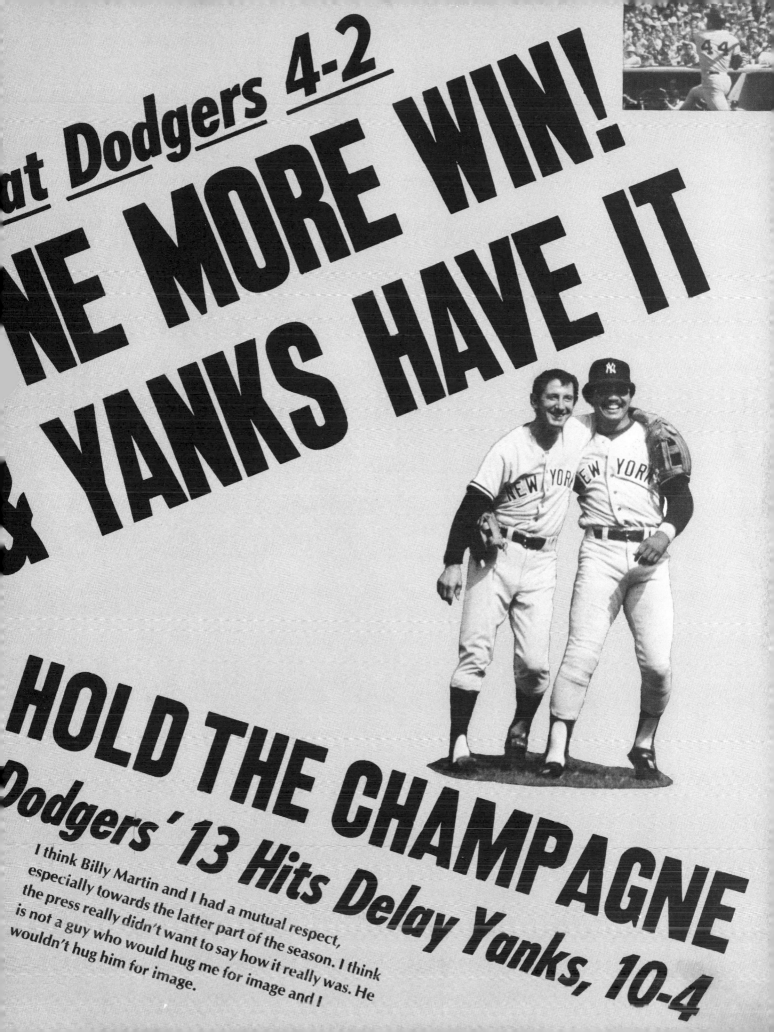

at Dodgers 4-2

NE MORE WIN!

YANKS HAVE IT

HOLD THE CHAMPAGNE

Dodgers' 13 Hits Delay Yanks, 10-4

I think Billy Martin and I had a mutual respect, especially towards the latter part of the season. I think the press really didn't want to say how it really was. He is not a guy who would hug me for image and I wouldn't hug him for image.

"Gettin' ready!"

BOOM!

#1

October 18

Homer #3 (overall) off Burt Hooton

BOOM

#2 #4 (overall) Elias Sosa October 18

I was very much in tune to swinging the bat and very much in harmony with being very exact.

"This is the final note that says it. That is my stamp for a home run."

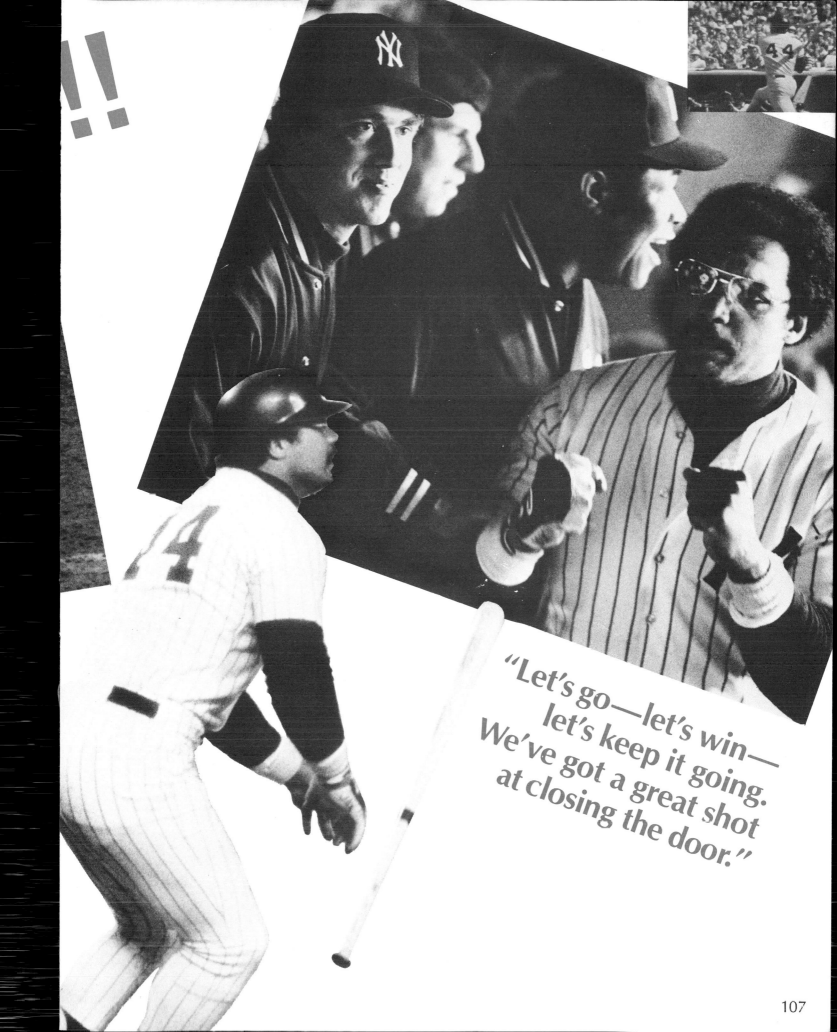

"Let's go—let's win—
let's keep it going.
We've got a great shot
at closing the door."

#3

#5 (overall)
October 18

I think I was able to hit the third
home run because Charlie Hough
was a knuckle ball pitcher. If he
hadn't been, he would have come
in and wasted a pitch or have
been a lot more cautious!

"It was very vogue (as they say in New York)
to be down on Reggie Jackson. And I
wanted to thank people for sticking with me."

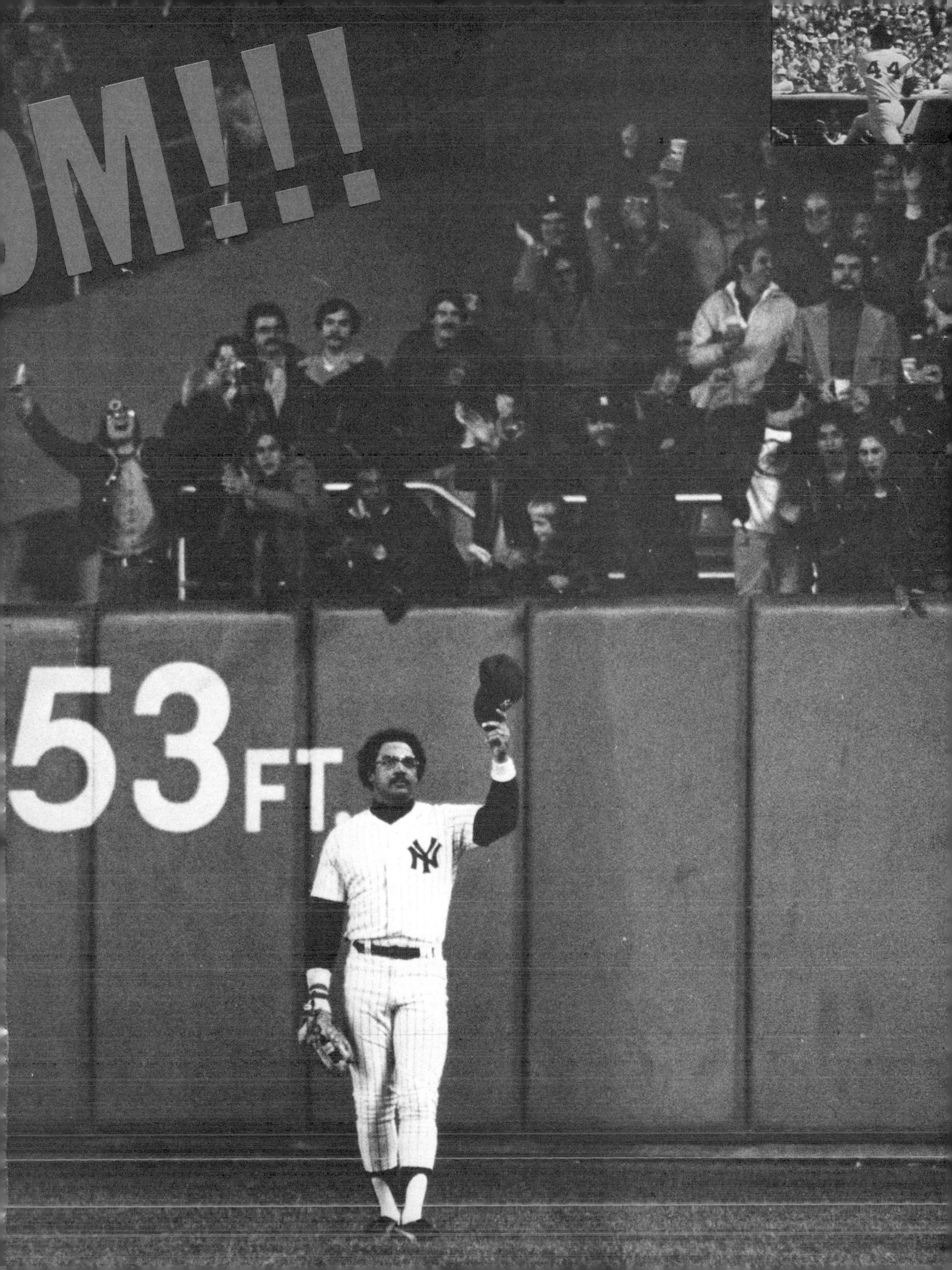
OM!!!
53 FT.
44

All I was doing was getting off that field. I just ran through the person and it came out like it was a block.

353 FT.

44

"Move over, O.J.
And Walter Payton."

REGGIE
REGGI
REGG

35³ FT.

Jackson Writes of Greatest Triump

44

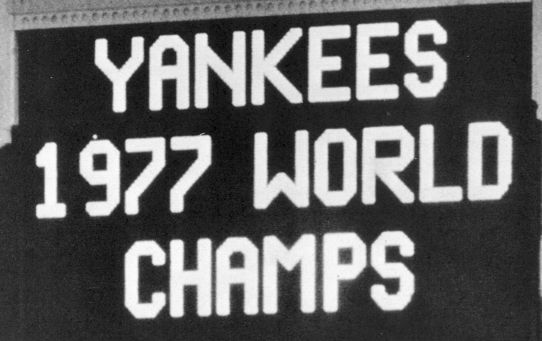

I was kidding Bowie Kuhn here, offering him some champagne. Remembering the 1974 World Series when I poured some on his coat and he said thanks but no thanks. Just having fun with each other.

People showing their excitement. I think the people of New York enjoy being champions more than anybody else in the country. They feel under pressure all the time because the city is projected as the biggest and the best. And when the team finally won, I think the whole city was proud and excited. It was personal to them. They shared in it.
That's what life is all about, isn't it? SHARING.

mmmmmmmmmmmmmmmmmmmmmmmmmm GOOOOOOOD!
and that ain't Campbell's soup!

"Nice guy— that Dad of mine!"

That is my father. You know, the season was so painful for him that he came to Yankee Stadium twice and was so hurt by the abuse I had to take that he never came back until the last game of the World Series. I think God was watching over him and me—allowing him to see those three home runs just for his personal satisfaction. For no other reason than just my Dad, I'm glad I hit the home runs. That was the most important thing that night—the most meaningful thing to me—that my Dad was there. It was the only World Series game he saw in 1977, the only game since August. Because he just got disgusted with the whole thing—he was very hurt by what was going on. Thank God he was able to share and enjoy that day.

Reggie hits his third home run—turns these double

4's and circles the bases to history.

JACKSON, REGINALD MARTINEZ "Reggie"   (OF)   #44

6-0, 200. Born on May 18, 1946 in Wyncote, Pennsylvania. Resides in Oakland, California. BL. TL. Single. College: Arizona State University.

Year	Club	AVG	G	AB	R	H	2B	3B	HR	RBI	BB	SO	SB
1966	Lewiston	.292	12	48	14	14	3	2	2	11	9	10	1
	Modesto	.299	56	221	50	66	6	0	21	60	15	71	3
1967	Birmingham	.293	114	413	84*	121	26	17*	17	58	44	87	17
	Kansas City	.178	35	118	13	21	4	4	1	6	10	46	1
1968	Oakland	.250	154	553	82	138	13	6	29	74	50	171*	14
1969	Oakland	.275	152	549	123*	151	36	3	47	118	114	142*	13
1970	Oakland	.237	149	426	57	101	21	2	23	66	75	135*	26
1971	Oakland	.277	150	567	87	157	29	3	32	80	63	161*	16
1972	Oakland	.265	135	499	72	132	25	2	25	75	59	125	9
1973	Oakland	.293	151	539	99*	158	28	2	32*	117*	76	111	22
1974	Oakland	.286	148	506	90	146	25	1	29	93	86	105	25
1975	Oakland	.253	157	593	91	150	39	3	36●	104	67	133	17
1976	Baltimore	.277	134	498	84	138	27	2	27	91	54	108	28
1977	New York	.286	146	525	93	150	39	2	32	110	75	129	17
	M.L. Totals	.268	1365	5373	891	1442	286	30	313	934	729	1366	198

Is that really the way I look?

PHOTO CREDITS

M. Grossbardt: II, VI-VII, 61, 65, 73, 76, 79

United Press: IV-V, 8, 10, 11, 13, 15, 17, 20, 24, 27, 35, 37, 38, 45, 51, 66-67, 77, 105, 106, 107, 117

Wide World: 16, 18, 19, 21, 23, 28-29, 30, 34, 38, 39, 47, 50, 52, 53, 54, 57, 58-59, 60, 63, 81, 82-83, 84, 85, 86, 87, 88, 89, 90, 93, 94, 95, 98-99, 104, 107, 108, 109, 110-111, 112-113, 115, 116

Camera 5: Ken Regan VIII-1, 41, 62, 100, 103, Curt Gunther 22, 23, Fred Kaplan 91, 96-97

Black Star: 36, 43
Time, Inc. 26
Sports Illustrated: 74, 114, 118
H. Humphrey: 120
Focus on Sports: 12, 14, 24, 31, 44, 46-47, 48, 49, 55, 56, 64, 75, 100, 102
Standard Brands Inc: Klaus Luca 98

Editor/Publisher/Art Director: Robert Kraus
Research: Martin Torgoff
Research Coordinator: F.C. Gove
Production: Steve Konopka
Director of Design: Nancy Etheredge
Jacket Design: Marilyn Rey
Book Design: Karen Bernath
Printed by Command Web Offset

We wish to thank the New York Yankees for their cooperation in furnishing us with material for this book.

We wish to thank Major League Baseball Film Division for permission to use the animated film strip of Reggie Jackson hitting a home run on top of the odd numbered pages.

We also want to thank the Daily News for the use of the headlines, the article on page 1, and the front page of October 19th of the Daily News on page 118.

Special thanks to Mrs. Clara Jackson for the use of her personal photographs.